PRAISE FOR *BIRDS AT THE POST OFFICE*

"These poems register precise impressions through carefully modulated language. Along the way, we encounter dodges and feints that display a wonderful range, and that consistently please with their quiet intensity."

— Baron Wormser, former Maine Poet Laureate

BIRDS AT THE POST OFFICE

RICHARD LEE ZURAS

Brandylane Publishers, Inc.
Publishing books since 1985

Copyright © 2020 by Richard Lee Zuras

All rights reserved. No part of this book may be reproduced in any form or by any electronic or mechanical means, or the facilitation thereof, including information storage and retrieval systems, without permission in writing from the publisher, except in the case of brief quotations published in articles and reviews. Any educational institution wishing to photocopy part or all of the work for classroom use, or individual researchers who would like to obtain permission to reprint the work for educational purposes, should contact the publisher.

ISBN: 978-1-951565-49-7

LCCN: 2020901448

Designed by Michael Hardison
Production managed by Grace Ball

Printed in the United States of America

Published by
Brandylane Publishers, Inc.
5 S. 1st Street
Richmond, Virginia 23219

brandylanepublishers.com

This book is dedicated to my wife, Kelly, and our sons, Everett and Holden, whose collective creative talents inspire me to stretch my own.

CONTENTS

BIRDS AT THE POST OFFICE	1
DROPPING MY SON AT COLLEGE	2
FIRST CHRISTMAS WITHOUT MY FATHER	3
FIRST DRUM LESSON	4
FONTANEL	5
GHOST	6
HAROLD'S & STACY'S	8
HIGHWAY BLUEBERRIES	9
HILL'S DENTAL CARE	10
HISTORY OF DANCE	12
MOM'S HOUSE	14
HOLOCAUST MUSEUM, WASHINGTON, D.C.	15
HOUSE HUNTING	16
HOW TO DIE HAPPY	18
IN HOSPITAL	19
IN THE CENTRE HOTEL	20
LINCOLN LOGS	21
LIVING IN THE RURAL	22
MR. G. & MS. L.	23
MY PRIMARY HEAVEN	24
ON A NABOKOVIAN LINE	25
OLD ORCHARD BEACH, MAINE	26
ON REMEMBERING MY BROTHER AND I ENDURED THE SAME UPBRINGING	28
POEM FOR MY ESTRANGED BROTHER	29
POEM FOR MY SON COMING HOME ON SPRING BREAK	30

POVERTY	*31*
PUNXSUTAWNEY PHIL	*32*
RADIO SILENCE	*33*
RED LOBSTER	*34*
RETURN OF LAKE AGASSIZ	*36*
RETURNING TO NORTHERN MAINE	*37*
ROGUE SOPRANO	*38*
SHALLOW GRAVE	*39*
ROOM SERVICE WAITER	*40*
SHOP TEACHER FROM HELL	*42*
SHOPLIFTING	*44*
SOMEWHERE IN MAINE	*45*
SOUTH OF INTERSTATE 10 *for John Wood*	*46*
SOUTHERN VIRGINIA WIDOW	*47*
STUDENTS AT A POETRY READING *for Kurt Brown*	*48*
TAPPING NEW ENGLAND	*49*
THE GAGGLE	*50*
TILLING THE EARTH	*51*
THE GREAT TOMATO WRECK	*52*
THREE ROLLS-ROYCES	*54*
UNIVERSITY LIFE	*56*
WATERVILLE, MAINE, OPERA HOUSE	*57*
WE GATHERED BERRIES	*58*
WEDDING GIFT, 1963	*59*
WEATHER GIRLS	*60*
WHAT ARE YOU GOING TO DO	*62*
WHAT CHEKHOV SAID ABOUT A MAN, A WOMAN, AND AN ASHTRAY	*63*

WHAT IF THE WEATHER CHANNEL FLIPPED	64
WHEN THE CASINOS CAME TO TOWN	65
WHEN I SPOT YOU	66
WHY I WRITE POEMS WHILE MY SONS REHEARSE MUMFORD & SONS	68
HOW ANIMALS ENTER POEMS	69
MISSPENT YOUTH IN THE MID-ATLANTIC	70
1979	71
1996	72
MAYBERRY	74
HAIKU CROWN	76-78
1. TEACAKE	76
2. HUSKY	76
3. NATIONAL GALLERY	76
4. SHAKESPEARE	76
5. ONE GUN, ONE BULLET	77
6. WHEELBARROW	77
7. HAIKU 1	77
8. HAIKU 2	77
9. HAIKU 3	78
10. PB&J	78
11. PRIMARY COLORS (YELLOW PINES)	78
12. POEM FOR MY SONS	78
NOT ANOTHER POEM ABOUT 22 GRAMS	79
ZURAS THE ETERNAL AS A SONNET	80
About the Author	83
Credits	85

BIRDS AT THE POST OFFICE

My friend Jerry is selling me Christmas stamps
Giant Santa faces painted like Disney cartoons

People behind me shuffling their L.L. Beans
Breathing like asthmatics waiting in line

For Jerry to finish his Christmas story
The little chickadees in his enormous backyard

How the chickadees swoop in and eat his berries
Then fly woozily into his picture windows

Jerry says it is too cold to affix the window stickers
And too snow-deep to pick all the berries

The asthmatics behind me are not asthmatics
That was wrong of me to suggest

But they do shuffle and breathe heavy
Like they think Jerry will hear them and stop

Boasting about his little drunk chickadee birds
So I refrain from egging him on how

Woozy the little chickadee birds must be
After slamming into his picture windows

Or telling him the little chickadee birds
Should try wearing tiny-bird helmets

Like Woodstock wore when Snoopy flew
Around as Red Baron in the Sopwith Camel

Instead I take my Santas home and stick them
To my picture windows. Twenty Santas facing

Outside. Facing the woozy-winter birds.

DROPPING MY SON AT COLLEGE

Daytime. It was January, snow had fallen
the previous day. Now came winter winds
blowing easterly, trucks belting down Route 1,
their cabs giraffing over the swirl,
my son and I low-gliding in a Nissan,
gleaning spare glimpses of daylight,
obliquely forming between water molecules—
frozen, swirling, whipping, drifting—
bouncing as we drifted, hitting drifts
as we searched through the atmosphere
for the road we still believed existed.
Each corridor of blown snow worse than the last.
In between drifts I ungripped the steering wheel
and together we ignored the noise—
skin unglueing from vinyl—
and I fiddled with the radio to calm
us. I attempted small talk
as if we were not driving a gauntlet,
as if we were not feeling like we had
simply gone too far to turn around. My son
beside me   his shape   still there
yet somehow ghostly—*as if he had himself
unglued,* first his hands, next his feet
from the rubber mat, my son lifted out obliquely,
searched for in the intermittent daylight.

FIRST CHRISTMAS WITHOUT MY FATHER

At Christmas each year my father
produced the same ornament anew
delayering countless dusty-blue tissues
from an old shoebox lettered in black:
Public Shoe Company. This, he said,
was his father's. It was a P-47 Thunderbolt
with fraying tape across its wings.
And what I remember is not my father's
face, nor the care he must have taken
nor the timbre of his voice, but the way
the thin wing-tape contained several
narrow spines of string, for strength.

My father's Lionels arrived today.
My mother had no use for them anymore
she wrote. And with that she had boxed
the old three-railed silver tracks, the straights
the curves, the switches, and the individually
wrapped interlocking railcars. My father's trolley
was there too, the type that lights up from inside
casting shadows of men reading the daily news
with grim morning faces, beneath worn
checked homburgs. She'd send the village later
she wrote, and had marked the box in black:
FRAGILE.

FIRST DRUM LESSON

I sit on a too-low Fender stool, in a small-town music store,
My feet pushing my knees into my chest, keeping time
As my guitarist son, a flautist by training, takes a drum lesson.
I thumb through a copy of *Drummer's World*, November issue
Deep in February, and my eyes gloss over the retro drums,
Blue pearlescence, a Country & Western set, exactly
Like my father's 1960s kit, the one he beat each weekend,
At the local Ramada, Sheraton, and Holiday Inn,

When he wasn't beating me, with his belt, a product of the era.
The kit I hoped to play, he sold for rent money to the brother
Of the kid who robbed me, my paper route money changing fists
Like a handshake.

         Poor is no one's fault,
         I had come to understand

A tumor, passed down through the blood, occasionally
Excised. I can hear enough to know my son has mastered
The basics, more than I ever learned, and in a matter of minutes.
What would my father do if he were here with me?
Would he sit and think so generationally?

Or use his ghostly shape to slip under the door, passing,
Through time and space, syncopating through the beat,
And take up residence on the small black stool, solemnly
Resting in the corner, just beyond my son's outstretched hands.

FONTANEL

Under new-mooned summer evenings
I visit my father like sleep
to plead with him to open his bone-dead eyes,
"Here, look, your grandson.
I will place him in your arms,
hold him there for you.
Encircle your dead fingers,
across his temples.
Feel his pulse now.
Your death is like the soft chasm, there in front,
Within his growing skull."

GHOST

My mother is a long-running widow
Going on ten years, or twenty.
Who bothers to keep count?
I am in her room, the sanctuary
Where my mother and father
Spent nights making whoopee,
As they actually called it,
When they were not worrying.

My mother has long since removed
My father, in a physical sense,
Yet his spirit lingers in the ravine
I spy, in the center of their bed.
I comment that mattresses
Should often be replaced,
Like people, every decade at least.
There is nothing wrong with it.

I cross to the window and pull
The shade, mother hides from the light.
Covers her eyes like a widow.
You might get stuck in there.
My mother places her hand
In the ravine, contemplates
Exactly what I have said.
It is clear mother believes this impression

Of my father, is all that she has left.
I lift the mattress and place another
Board under the ravine. Next year I will
Lift the mattress again, and place another.
Years on, I will finally lift the mattress
As light as air, worn brass coil springs
A dusting of cotton-frayed material,
Two wondrous ghosts in a ravine.

HAROLD'S & STACY'S

Small town
Lunchtime
Order of mashed

Potatoes
The local home
Grown food

Harold cooks
Stacy serves proud
You eat

What you can
Leave
The rest

Stacy takes it
Personally
Takes it away

Your first
Experience
Small-town lunch.

HIGHWAY BLUEBERRIES

Logging trucks hug the first row, spewing thick black smoke
Carcinogens like atoms, a DNA double helix of death.
The fog collects like trash on the roadside,
Before organizing in uniformed teams to descend
On this acre of highbush Maine blueberries. Families
Have assembled in cohorts of threes and fours: the Amish,
The Lutherans, and the Atheists. Children play chess
On the human-sized board, watching, and pointing,
At the smoke as it dissipates, fallout falling in between

Row after row of green and blue berries. New buds mingle
With full, berries straining to be reached in the thickness
Of untrimmed hedgerows. The smoke settles into physical
Soot atop straw hats and fingernails, the berries loose
In hands, filling bags and the footfall below. No one picks
The fat blueberries nearest the road. Another logger rolls by.

HILL'S DENTAL CARE

Over pot pies and a side of molasses beans
I told my wife our Siberian Husky
Is in love, not with the Rottweiler next door,
But with her bag of Hill's Prevention Diet
T/D Dental Care. My wife shook her head,
Asked is that how I spent my day again,
Analyzing the simple actions of the world
Around me, then typing them into neat cubes.
Rather than admit I had or would write a poem
Likely entitled Hill's Dental Care…
I finished my molasses beans and prattled on.
Here is the thing, I said, she had this one T/D
She deemed more important than the rest,
Kept taking it in and out of the house through
The sliding glass door I left open all day.
A Husky-sized doggy door, my wife said,
And I nodded yes, spreading my hands just so.
I placed a T/D in my teeth, demonstrated
How our Siberian carried it to and fro, drooling.

My wife said nothing, slowly finished her molasses
Beans. Here is the kicker, I said, rubbing my hands
Together like Gary Soto's Orange-Fire image, trying
To create that moment of heat Terrance Hayes
Says all poems need. I got down on all fours,
Our Siberian jabbing her cold nose into my armpits,
I started to dig at the carpet, let my tongue fall free.
I said out back in the snow she was digging like this,
Furiously, all the way to the ground, trying to find
That special T/D, bring it back to the surface. I placed
My wallet next to me, sniffed at it, then I pretended
The wallet was not there. Went back to digging, ass
In the air. Just like that, I said, as if she could not accept
It was not down there. When I came back up, my wife
And Siberian were nowhere in sight. I stood up and looked
Out back, through the makeshift doggie door. Breathed
The visible night air, watched our Siberian reach in
And out of her chasm, her T/D faithfully by her side.

HISTORY OF DANCE

Funny thing is they have all seen *Grease*
And half of them have watched the sing-along
and most covet the dance scene
With the fake Dick Clark. But here is your
Teenager and mine, getting dressed up
For the big dance, full-length mirrors
Dusted off and stolen, from their long naps,
Neckties pulled uneasily into full Windsor
Knots, whimsical socks give a wink
Below painted Chuck Taylors, or heels
As tall as you remember them.
Makeup, perfume, designer cologne,
Teeth brushed with a purpose, with intent,
A new pack of breath mints, a bow,
And a sprig of heather in their hair.
Limos are rented in southwest Nebraska
Classic cars rev up and leave their cocoons,
Dinners in mixed groups, desserts consumed
In fancy restaurants, or backyard gazebos.

Principals, even teachers from shop sporting
Fancy kerchiefs and checkered tied bowties.
Inside, the gym, or the historic hotel,
Ballrooms filled with blown balloons
And crepe, the DJ watches a laptop
Replete with two two-dimensional LP
Records, spinning, songs ripping off
One another, merging through twin PA
Speakers, poled and middled on the rented
Parquet dance floor. Phones are held
In lieu of hands, notes passed, without touch.
Someone adjusts a tie, someone reapplies
A cherry lip, a stray toe taps, a head bobs.
The gravity of the walls too strong, inertia
Studied in real time, and time itself rolls
From eight to nine and ten, eleven finds
Twelve, requisite pumpkin jokes implored,
Teens exploding into the night, single
Beds prepped and waiting. Nothing left
But to pop the balloons, roll up and save
The crepe paper, return the unused dance floor.

MOM'S HOUSE

Her front/side/back yards should have been a clue:
Overgrown trees, branches hugging the low roof,
Drainpipes half in the ground, a history of rainwater
Disappeared into walls, an acre of land like prehistoric
Gardens of hell. Her front door unable to perform,
Finding itself an unwilling U-Haul box mover. Inside,
The stench of smoke, off-brand Lysol, used cat litter.

Outside you sat in the car, our two boys belted.
Inside I sifted through the residue of life, a world
Of hoarding curses the living, and the dead. A moment,
Time ushers in shame, the here the now, all that is left
Of a life spent like money, like the empty box in the corner
A place to put everything as if it belongs somewhere,
The cat fits in the box, the box on my lap. Watch the box purr.

HOLOCAUST MUSEUM, WASHINGTON, D.C.

My mother was precancerous then, willing
to care for our two young sons for an afternoon.
My wife and I stole that time, setting off
for Washington's new Holocaust Museum.
I remember entering the museum, how it seemed
like a Frank Lloyd Wright effect, the tunnel-
like entrance blooming into a well-lit lobby.

We waited,

knowing where they were taking us,
somehow correct and incongruous
all at once. We grasped our fake passports
and rode an elevator with a somber man
who worked a job seldom discussed. How
would one advertise that job?

When we emerged upstairs I had no idea what to expect—
and I saw children all around me, grouped on field trips,
and I saw educators pointing at names and images,
and I saw children clutching their fake passports,
and I heard faint crying from a video screen sunken

in the corner.

The line swept over us, we propelled along
the timeline. Fully aware we would not be asked
to surrender
even the fake passports
that we would stare at, later,
on the well-lit subway, wondering where
these souvenirs would end up. Would be remembered.

HOUSE HUNTING

The baby is riding my shoulders up high
Jostling his hips and pointing wet fingers at the seller
As if she has something to hide

I'm pointing her way too,
In the basement where the bricks won't tuck,
In the corners where the floors divot and lean.

My wife glares at me and hugs her chest,
Like we better buy this one or else—

Maybe the antebellum plainness of it all?
The men and women who have whiled life here
Add up over time

Into nothing.

The baby resumes kicking my kidneys,
While I rub windows for traces of heating oil,

And open the toilet tanks and skim for sediment,
Flip on the lights to check for electrical strains.
The baby reaching and pointing all the while.

My wife and the seller look like sisters,
Measuring the countertops and vaulted ceilings,
Like the movers are at the doorjamb.

The seller *mentions* her prostate cancer
As if she's pointing out a carpet stain.
My wife holds her at the wrist,

I think again, they could be sisters…
"I thought only men contract that," I say.
"Some men get breast cancer," she replies.

I shift my weight over my heels,
Ask her to sign the disclosure form,
Mindful of the irony,
The growing weight on my back.

HOW TO DIE HAPPY

My grandfather died on New Year's Eve 1962
After gorging on a tenderloin steak
The kind he used to deliver
In a black & white panel truck
Zuras Poultry & Meats painted
In black & white or red white & blue.
Because he once was a marine.

In old photographs he seemed to enjoy
Living in his black & white world—
My Czech grandmother, his proud wife,
Astride him, dressed to the nines
In the latest black & white flapper wear.

My mother's father never ate steak,
Or at least not on the night he died.
   (we never spoke of his death, only alcohol)
In the lone photo I possess he is in color,
Smiling, his curly steel hook deep in ice,
Hauling its weight on his back, upstairs.
Upstairs, they await his arrival—
Perhaps it is a penthouse apartment
Angels awaiting a block of ice
To place in front of their fans.
A velvet couch, my grandfather
Reclining, the sweat on his lovely
Brow dissipating into cool air.

IN HOSPITAL

I pour myself out of the La-Z-Boy
Like I have poured and grilled flapjacks
All these humid, cockroach-filled summer months.
I find our dog where you put her
Near the front door
In mid-June.
By rote we circle her collar
Around her neck and stride
One by one into the hot August son.
I have filled these heatfire months
Since you disappeared
With mindless BBC comedies
From decades gone by.
Our dog knows the drill
Left turns around the neighborhood
Like a retired NASCAR driver. Circling.
I don't mind the time to think. In hospital.
Those crazy Brits with their diction.
I create a sitcom for BBC while we circle
Passing by our unlit house time and again.
You in hospital, me like a fop
Off to visit you on a lazy Sunday morn.
Perhaps for tea? What's for tea? Crazy Brits.
I arrive like they do on the telly
Stylish hat and suit coat in summer
A thicket of green grapes in tow.
Perhaps we have had a wee row
And I hem and haw in the chair
To your right, the camera off right.
A two-shot, the grapes in the foreground
The two of us deeply focused in background.

IN THE CENTRE HOTEL

Room service waiters fold linen napkins
Into lotus flowers and flying nuns. Dressed
In copper-buttoned navy/white uniforms,
Shoes, patent leather, black, spit-shined.
The men talk of baseball and prize fights,
The bravado of friendship. The line cooks
Nearby notice first, the rollaway bed wheeled
Like a gurney past the cold line, pastrami
Sandwiches, Cobb salads, black mousse.
The wheels squeak a song, the gurney struggling
Around the corner, the room service waiters,
Their flying nuns halted in half fold, pink and crisp,
The gurney bumps their folding table, a glimpse
Under the sheets, an elderly man, clearly dead,
His dignity nowhere to be found. Outside,
Off the loading dock and into a hotel van.
The rumors followed quickly in his wake.
A public official, said the front desk staff,
Food & Beverage swore he was a senator.
The woman, consensus, a call girl, the death,
A heart attack. The room service waiters
Discussed who had served his room, folded
Flying nuns and lotus flowers in pink and white.

LINCOLN LOGS

There's a slice of light in my twins' playroom.
A wedge, a shaft, no more than two by two,
knifing across their well-worn blue carpet.
They avoid the light like fire, pushing

Ma and Pa's Lincoln Log cabin from its path
encroaching, as though the heavily varnished logs
might combust, spontaneously, plastic green roof-
smoke rising, escaping the plastic red brick chimney.

The tiny horse and its tiny buggy running scared,
the tiny covered wagon leaping and dancing
across uncharted prairies, leaving behind
two stern figures to fend for themselves.

LIVING IN THE RURAL

A helicopter chops the air and folks
drop everything, groceries, beers, jaws.
They look up (they stare). Back in my
Childhood, Dulles International Airport,
Such a helicopter did not raise a flinch.

The Concorde did. The noise-laden crane
daily buzzed our tiny trailer, my mother
held on to our green GE stovetop while

the jumbo Air France rumbled the sky—
its second deck alive with Gershwin.
"Imagine that," Mother would say,
"Rhapsody in Blue."

Still holding the oven handle.

I imagine a drink in my left hand
An MGM actress on my right arm
my college textbooks rhapsodic
across the grand piano. The Steinway
replete with slinky shadows of cocktail
waitresses fresh from central casting,
slinging slo-gins into quilted, crystal
stems. Frank Sinatra clears his worn throat,
nudged by the ladies, he sings…

MR. G. & MS. L.

The filmstrip stopped, our sixth-grade fun
Over, lights snapped on, our rubber bands,
Unfolded paper clips, exposed: little
Warriors. Our makeshift bow & arrows.

Led by our tender young ears,
Back to our classroom
For Mr. G. in all his glory.
We knew the drill:

The blackboards filled with his anger.
What he wanted to say
He instead wrote down.
Burned it into our brains.

Our pencils unable to keep time
With his wrath. He wrote for miles,
One blackboard into the next.
Ms. L, always sure to tousle our hair,

Walking around us, diffusing
The air. Squeezing our shoulders,
Offering a cooling hand amidst fire.
All of us hoping Mr. G would exhaust his love.

MY PRIMARY HEAVEN

In my heaven I am not married
Or a father or an estranged brother
Or an orphan, or gray, old, and wrinkled.

I am of indeterminate age, but young
Sitting on the sunshine sands of
An indeterminate playground.

Every toy I ever owned or coveted
Is within my grasp, lined up, encircling
Me. Clean, whole, in good working order.

Not forever lost in a hall closet. G.I. Joe
Stolen by my best "friend" to forever hang
On a clothesline, half burned by his Bic.

The Superman action figure is mine.
I own it. Red plastic cape supple but firm.
My Batman's Robin is name brand
The Star Trek transporter spins correctly
Hiding Spock behind the black curtain
Where he joins Kirk in his spandex yellow top.

ON A NABOKOVIAN LINE

Nabokov wrote, "And sometimes trains would cry in the monstrously hot and humid night with heartrending and ominous plangency, mingling power and hysteria in one desperate scream." He was in Pennsylvania when he offered this rather detailed description, or rather Humbert Humbert was, and as he had implied, it was raining. I take it to have been July, deep in, or perhaps August. But here where I live, far up north, where humidity seals in cold not heat, the air is indeed monstrous at night, in the lungs, the nostrils, the esophagus, threatening to freeze rows of teeth and tips of tongues. Through this tight air, southbound train cars couple on dead-end tracks, open air haulers of newly felled trees buckle against closed-in coal cars, merging power with power. True, there is, depending on one's distance, something of a scream in the night. A disheartening primal screech, as if two powerful and bestial animals had engaged out of hysterical desperation. Like Humbert and Lolita.

OLD ORCHARD BEACH, MAINE

Who would have thought a forest
Of ancient pine trees would grow
Half a mile from the beach
Reaching so high that each needle
Slowly floats, like a tiny hang glider
Turning and tumbling ever so gently
Before resting on a bed of sand
Covered in green and brown needles.

And who could have imagined a sandy beach
Right at the precipice of a thousand-acre
Apple orchard. The apples long gone—
Replaced by clapboard houses, pedestrians
In flip-flops, hands sticky with cotton candy
And salt water, salt air, hand-pulled salt taffy.

Once did pirates look through a spyglass
At green apples on green-leaved trees.
Now? Mothers look up at their children
High above, rocked to and fro, waving,
On an amusing, three-dollar-a-ride pirate ship.

The Palace Playland with its Whac-A-Mole
And its nostalgic long-track Skee-Ball
Rests on a tract that was once a cemetery
Or perhaps the apple pickers' barracks.
Imagine those pickers now, rising up from
Their deathbeds, the lights and whirls
Of the arcade, the dollar changers, the pinball
And the noisy plastic bubble housing tiny plastic
Hockey players passing a tiny plastic puck
The size of a Granny Smith apple core.

There they are, still wearing their pickers' bibs,
Their pickers' overalls, the long day's work
Staining the blue denim in a sweet and sickly rot.
The cashier hands them each a quarter, to entice.
The bells and whistles beckon, a quick glance
At the Skee-Ball, the quarters quickly stowed,
Deep in pockets, each picker keeping a bony hand
Across the opening seam, protecting the day's pay.

ON REMEMBERING MY BROTHER AND I ENDURED THE SAME UPBRINGING

Our banana bicycle seats pressed foam under plastic
So hard our crotches ached before we rode a mile.

Out past the 7-Eleven where we lost our quarters
In the hungry mouth of the pinball machine

We stopped, kickstanded our Huffy bikes,
And admired the aroma of the nectar we sought.

The Virginia honeysuckle and onion grass,
The caterwaul of murderous crows, and magpies.

We summered there, sunning in white tank tops,
The ozone above us burning away. Sometimes,

A sleep came over us. A momentary peace.
An awareness of the theory of escape. Other

Times we were content to pull the honey-stem,
Its bended end exposing the pearl of gold.

POEM FOR MY ESTRANGED BROTHER

Remember, brother, when we took the bus
To Tyson's Corner or Skyline Mall or the State
Theater and we pooled our change, purchased
Theater-size boxes of Sno-Caps and Now & Laters?
Slingshot them, with thick newspaper rubber bands,
The discs and cubes sluicing off the silver screen,
The pair of us hunching down in our front row seats?

Those theater screens were enormous, remember?
Eighty feet wide & looking back, no wonder no one
Noticed us. Tapped our shoulders. Asked us to leave.

We would walk the entire mall, yapping away
Like adults, discussing the unintelligible world
Of James Bond. 007. Remember the one set in Greece?
That woman, my first screen crush. We both wanted
To be Bond, and your name being James, you lorded
That over me, your forest green collar flipped cool
Your Timex watch, a ballpoint pen in your shirt pocket,
Remember? I have borrowed your pen, my brother. I
Wonder, will you stand tall and take it back from me?

POEM FOR MY SON
COMING HOME ON SPRING BREAK

When you were eight I brought you
        home to eat lunch
When you did not want to miss me
        and your mother
When you were five I took you to a
        party with swords
When you got upset at your brother
        I had to separate you
When you were separated you got mad
        because you were separated
When you sang in the chorus at school
        I thought you would faint
When you graduated high school
        you were taller than me
When you left home for college
        we were aware you left
When you read this poem I will know
        you are no longer a child.

POVERTY

It is a terrible thing, memory
When it hits you in the shoe aisle
Of your local Macy's or Nordstrom.
You are buying dress shoes for your son:

A high school choral concert, winter show.
You have placed six pairs of black shoes
on the bench, having not looked at prices.

Your son is shoehorning his feet
Into one pair after the other
And you can't get the image
Out of your mind.

Winter, you are eight years old.
Your mother ties a plastic shopping bag
Into a knot around your beaten shoe.
The bag is beige and smells of the oil can
It once held in the shed. The cashier is polite

Compliments your son before placing
His new shoes in a free canvas bag. Your son swings
The bag as he walks through the garden of perfect
Mannequins—Izod golf shirts over pleated khaki pants.
Tennis rackets and mint juleps in hand.

PUNXSUTAWNEY PHIL

NOAA states that old Phil is correct
About forty percent of Groundhog Days.
How did we devise such a holiday?
And who sees their shadow and thinks,
More winter. Six weeks. Less winter.

When I see my shadow, I know I am alive,
When I don't, I just assume it anyway.
Perhaps NOAA should state we are all right
Sixty percent of Groundhog Days
By assuming Punxsutawney Phil is wrong.

I once knew a gentle man that said
*I can call the flip of a coin wrong
Each and every time without fail.*
Obviously I asked him,
Doesn't that mean you can also call it?

The gentle man was also named Phil,
From Wichita, Kansas. He replied:
*I am always sure I am correct
And astonished when I am not.* If you study
Punxsutawney Phil's eyes, he thinks the same.

RADIO SILENCE

My father never forgave me
For not speaking to him
In the silences that occupy
Our lives. Teenage angst

Haunts my young son
He does not speak to me.

I bark at my typewriter
Its ancient keys: QWERTY
Cobbling words together
In one more inane poem

My rather brilliant idea
To tell my young son
About the horror of regret
And why he is so silent

With me over cold cereal
When we pass in the hallway
When he chooses strangers
Who will all disappear

From his life I will be gone
One day I told him about
This chasm of silent regret
Apologies for the burden

RED LOBSTER

I am writing this poem at my desk
Under my Pinocchio lamp owned since
Childhood, trying to remember the name
Of the restaurant where we ate Saturdays
Twice a month to get my father's mother
Out of her house. I know my title is wrong,
A placeholder, for this was the 1970s,
And though I clearly remember Gifford's,
My mother would not allow my father's
Mother to follow us for Saturday dessert.

I can see Philly, my grandmother, clear
As I see my blue fountain pen, her hair
Tidied beneath a too-thin Russian scarf,
The kind she bought at Ben Franklin's.
Her off-white pearl necklace strung
Loosely around her neck, an occasional
Pearl cracked, its presence a reminder
To my mother that my father was too good
For a rural Marylander who pronounces
Washington with an R. The restaurant

Is visible even in the low light of my lamp.
Families like ours—women and men
With two kids and a widowed mother
In tow. A jukebox in the corner, scratchy
Records two years out of date, fake Tiffany
Lamps and a busy cigarette machine. A cup
Of broken crayons and too-cute children's
Placemats for the mothers to draw on,
Avoiding mother-in-law countenance.

    The widows pick at their food, pick at
    The children. (Lums. The name was Lums.)
    My grandmother picking through her ancient
    Coin purse, counting dimes like valuables.

RETURN OF LAKE AGASSIZ

    I returned with my wife to where the floods
of ninety-seven had wiped out the whole
of our neighborhood. Where all the houses
had peeled down like clapboard banyan trees

        and we stood in caked mud, careless children
        wearing our Easter shoes an hour past church.
        Our Siberian sniffed as we cruised the rubbled streets,
        stood where kitchens had hummed with baking,

water-stained photographs blowing across
the un-mowed berms. Images of baptisms,
graduations, weddings, births. Divorced friends
houses gone, marked by ribbons, nailed

into dying oaks, having barely survived
the return of the ancient lake, while the homes
        they shaded revealed, imperfections. Our house
        emptied of its contents, stiffly hoped to move

        to a local museum, to die forever as an example
        of early steel structure. My wife took one last tour
        inside and with a shale in her palm gauged its metal:
        Do not tear this house down.

RETURNING TO NORTHERN MAINE

I wanted to write about barns collapsing
On the forty-mile stretch from Houlton
To Presque Isle, the west side of Route 1
Then the east, assuming Route 1 as straight
And narrow, but the television is on
At the end of the bar I did not pass.
A local has broken the dark contract
Of silence to alert his fellow drinkers
That the television is pointing out
The fact that a gator, twenty-plus-footer,
I would hazard, has staked out the 18th
Green, slithering as if it were a snake.
A tiny golf ball comic next to its mouth,
A frightened egg. Floridians are funny
So the ESPN commentators rightly laugh
At the octogenarian in the background,
Hands on checkered hips, waiting for the gator
To play through already. I turn back to my
Notes, pictures of failing barns snapped
On my phone. The snow-capped concave
Roofs weighty under the craggle, the empty
Spaces within. I picture the horses, the grain,
The potatoes they once housed. Order another.

ROGUE SOPRANO

He trolleys in, lamenting his bookbag—
drops the innumerable pictographs, splays
them, honestly, rolling the floor like ovoids,
as if our Maine mudroom were a
paralytic chapel.

"Mr. Sipe keeps telling our whole grade,
'There's a rogue soprano hiding out in the altos.'"
He smiles—

There is a certain hokiness when my son imitates
his teachers—an affection not lost on either party.
He is vamping now…

A tuft of auburn hair will not find
agency (his head blossoming inside and out).
I coil it with my fingertips. He is just now
thirteen. He no longer woos me.
His impertinence startles

but I stow his brief attentiveness, a
Krugerrand (fatuously) into my pocket.
Soon his voice will be hijacked by the gods and devils
of arduous hormones. (For now, a partition.)
        This wanton glitch.

SHALLOW GRAVE

My wife's belly like a giant navel orange
Provides the racetrack. The technician
This time, is not a robot. She circles
The pregnant belly to the left, as race

Car drivers do. I tell the human tech
The doctor has already buried our fetus
In a shallow grave. The bell racetrack has

dried and the tech shakes the tube and spooges
more purple-pink goo. I watch the belly button
quiver. The gooey gunk looks like candy
working itself loose on a taffy puller. Slow

heartbeat, my wife says. The tech adjusts the screen
and nudges a few buttons. The heartbeat is like
a grade school band: nervous, ducking, unsure.

The song is older than birdsong and slow. My fifteen-
year-old's, she says, was slower than this. The human
tech smiles and regales my wife with stories. What a
pain in the ass that kid is sometimes. Teenagers,

she says. I'm thinking how much I love that kid.

ROOM SERVICE WAITER

You've gone and done it now. You've sliced
open your wrist and it's right up the vein line
full of grist, gory as hell, cut from the lip
of the wide-mouthed, hand-blown Mexican glass,
replete with your blood juice. No one saw it happen.
Of course. You are a room service waiter
in a mocking polka dot, black bow tie
and cumberbund and the pink-paper-lined
bamboo serving tray slurps the dripgush
of your blood. You wrap a semi-clean, thirty-six-inch
tablecloth around your wrist and watch white
go crimson. Now the dumbfounded cabbie has you,
your good hand clutching the taxi voucher.
He is eyeballing you in the rearview. Your indiscretion
is one he's seen too many times. You're downtown
and on line at Mercy Hospital. Intake
is slow

people judging you as having come from a swank party—
cumberbund, black bow tie. You with your buttoned-up appearance.
Black market shoes and hair clipped off the ear-line.
You've remembered to remove your nametag,
and that was a mistake. The doctor is tired, waves to
invites you in. She cleans the grist-wound right smack
in front of you   and you watch   with   detached
interest. She works it like a sewer grate,
asks if you've just tried to kill yourself
at the precise moment your vagal response
kicks in. You hear her say *oh dear* and she helps you
stand back up, and the oxygen mask tastes *good*,
really, and you can see it bothers her that you fell.
You pull the mask off and tell her no, not on a night
when people are ordering steaks. She smirks. At you.

SHOP TEACHER FROM HELL

Not that four-fingered guy you had
That sincerely warned you how
To keep your digits pulsing
After the circular saw boomeranged
Its sandy circle of death
Across your eyebrows.

This was the shop teacher I had
So that you did not. This was
The shop teacher that told us
Our grades with a smirk and a wink:
You are lucky my wife served
Meatloaf last night when I did grades
Or you would have failed.

Let me give the only examples
You need. One: In leatherworking
The shop teacher from hell
Showed me how to wet bevel
The edge of my coaster
By beveling the tool right through
The edge of my coaster.

Two: After ruining my coaster
And walking away as if he had not
The shop teacher from hell
Crossed my path one fine day
And I showed him my leather
Keychain made under his fine eye.

I can't believe that has held up
All these years and it really was
Not made well was it?

If it makes you feel better
I was prepared for
The shop teacher from hell
By my previous
Shop teacher from hell
Who told me to grade my own
Spot welded metal box
And when I said A
He laughed at me
And said D at best.

SHOPLIFTING

Rectangles of chewing gum oddly named Trident
Protrude from the orange stripes of my tube sock.
The gum-weight rectangles bulging at the fibers
Of my sock, made too clear by overhead fluorescents.

Mother finds me at the precipice of the register
Places her cat food on the conveyor belt and stares.
God's light overhead, her eyes meet mine.
Like a cop she looks me over, or:

Gives me the once-over like store security.
And I am sweating bullets
              I could fill her six-shooter
Then the six-pack of Trident leaps out.

(I am ten or eleven with a criminal mind
Plotting a fortune turned one nickel at a time)
The little rectangles inside their rectangle packs
Spill out as one with a noise bigger than—

(Run? Hide? Kick it? I am positive I am eleven)
I pick it up as if it was as simple as a coin drop.
(In my mind I am leaping onto the conveyor belt
Like Chuck Norris or Bruce Lee.)

In Mother's mind she places me in multiple brown
Paper bags, in small pieces, stows me in the cart:
Turned wheels scrape, screech across the lot, shouting
My name aloud again and again as if for the first time.

SOMEWHERE IN MAINE

The road sign read DEER: HIGH HIT AREA
Yet still I missed. He came left to right
From east to west across a straight on Interstate 95
Where I was cruising along in my tin machine
On down to Orono to pick up my college son.

Obviously no one saw the thing, dirty snowbanks
Lining the highway's shoulders, makeshift bumpers
Serving as guardrails, but too low to curtail deer.
He came right off the right headlight of a gray
Ford Flex, did not hit, missing the built-in irony,
Ran like a deer, no other way to explain it, was gone
Before I reached him. I braked, amazed I saw, reacted,
My silver hair likely standing on end as I checked
Every mirror and saw nothing. He saw me, clearly,
And I picture him later that evening, settling down
With his deer friends in the shallow woods west
Of the interstate. All of them swapping their stories
Disembarked from their speed, relaxed, one deer
Telling the others how he almost hit a Ford and a
Nissan, an older deer says something about proliferation,
How they need to take some of us out, control our population.

SOUTH OF INTERSTATE 10
for John Wood

He came to our student parties,
The poet in his seersucker suit:
The poet in his mint green pants
Serving his mint green juleps.
A youthful grin belied imperfect
Teeth, hair tousled like youth
His laughter infectious…

He held the Gods of poetry
Within him, reciting lines at will:
St. Vincent Millay, Joyce, et al.
Stirring the juleps with homemade
Sugar-swizzle sticks. What fun we had,
all from elsewhere, thrust into his world,
Louisiana, Land of Zydeco and Mardi Gras

Parades. The poet sitting on the counter,
Drink in hand, legs crossed and kicking
Like a child pleased with himself, watching us
Drink his nectar. The poet in his seersucker suit
wondering if we understood. Outside looking in,
we wondered if he was teaching us poetry,
or crafting a cult of poets.

SOUTHERN VIRGINIA WIDOW

Amidst fat honeysuckle and gold bees
our two lawns aligned, carpeted terra firma,
my brother striking gray-shale stones
off the end of his yellow Wiffle bat.

Her second-story window glass bore out
like honeycomb. Our bittersweet laughter rose up—
then her garden hose, suddenly on us, like a riot.
Later, Dad admonished *her* with our youth

(inside he scolded *us* like milk). The widow's
family, he traduced, traced back to the Civil War.

Mother couldn't reconcile for us the word
war with the word *civil*—we knew civil—from church.

And we knew we looked different from the widow,
Acted different, smelled different.
We were northerners—New South, invading
Old South. We were death to her, Dad said.

Cajoling us, he wielded his glass cutter knife,
Windows to repair, he hassled us into her yard.
Aside from the glass, the widow's grass looked like ours—
Gold honeysuckle and fat swarming bees.

STUDENTS AT A POETRY READING
for Kurt Brown

We brought them here at night.
Not under the cover of darkness,
But under the cover of grades.
Excused from quizzes and classes,
As if education could be substituted
    For education.

Look at that one there with her hair
And that boy why don't they listen?
That poet speaks of death
    And other things.

When he says *sex* their bodies *perk*
As if all one needed to reach them
Was a man humping a car
    The *windshield* no less.

The poet speaks of wow and flutter,
Wonders why they don't laugh
In the correct places.
The poet speaks of aging   the students   wander
    Mindful of the time.

They are looking at each other
Through a mirror.

TAPPING NEW ENGLAND

Of all the beautiful sap trees I have tapped
The hard maple has notably run the boldest,
The soft maple a proud second bleeder
And the box elder seldom worth the bother.

But the line of birches that rings my acreage
Provides the nectar I chose for thirty years
To bathe my short and tall stacks. Gathering
Is easier as I age, the air springing warmer,

Bringing my pale buckets out two weeks
Early, the spy of grass after harsh winters
The trade-off for a lessening of sugar. Nearer
Town the young ones are educated and nervous

Full of worry beyond their experience. Afraid
We will tap out. At seventy-six, I am an old sap
With dogs and no kin, selfish with my world.
But I do worry the pear thrip, and have fought

The good fight against the forest tent caterpillar.
Still, I lay my lines where gravity assists me,
Place my buckets and handstitched sacks.
Three generations have taught me how to hammer,

No need for a drill, my grandfather's hand-forged
Spiles fill these woods like new growth. The birches
Too lacking for a second tap, speeds up the process.
Up goes the buckets. My dogs nowhere in sight.

THE GAGGLE

Of ducks is crossing the narrow road
Separating the hospital from the pond.
The pond is existential,

More a GPS suggestion of a pond,
The diameter full of snow
The circumference ringed with remnants

Of snow, slush, ice, crust, water
Vapor, the evaporation of snow,
Algae under, frozen, duck shit, frozen

Bread thrown with prayers for the living
As well as the dead, the sick, the infirm.
The well-wishers, the children's noses

Pressed to hospital window glass
The ducks unaware of the burdens
They carry, the momentary break

From unending death two floors up.
The newly born a floor below. Cars
Carry the newly grieved or temporary

Reprieve back home. A moment's break,
A light blare of the horn, the mallard
Unflinching, the murder of crows looks on.

TILLING THE EARTH

We cut an untraceable path through the broken,
burrowed field of unharvested soybeans,
behind the house your parents built to live and die
within, in order to witness our coming nuptials.
In the gentle recesses of my vivid memories
stands not my vows, forged by my pen, alone,
under a velvet rope lamp
in an unused storage room,
nor the way the sunlight beams
through the twisted vines of the earth
we now till in our Sunday shoes.
But the way my father and my mother
seem trapped in their own wedding photo.
My father's eyes beating at the sides of the frame,
and my mother's dress threatening to catch fire
from the heat I caused in her womb.
Note how the onlookers pretend they do not see
    the consequential bump I made there.
Perhaps with my head, or the protrusions of my feet.

THE GREAT TOMATO WRECK

My friend Tom used to haul eighteen-wheelers
Out of roadside ditches near the Thames.

An expert in third axle recoveries
Tom was a drinker: ale, black rum, red wine.

He drank and spoke of his apprentice years,
About the first time he flipped a rig, solo.

A tomato truck, 40,000 pounds of juicy Romas
Forced off the road midwinter by a snowplow.

He spoke of the traffic jam, backed up around
The Thames, curled off into the peal of side streets.

All eyes were on me. That always brought me
To the time I parked in a snowbank, cocksure

My Jeep Wrangler's low-low-gear
Could overcome anything, as advertised.

That young man laughed as I spewed snow
Hooked up a chain and yanked me

Out of the ditch, my front axle forever askew.
Tom loved it, saw my ignorance as pleasure.

Said I must have looked like a kitten
Yanked out of a litter box by the scruff.

We traded our stories as if they were new
The way you do with old friends.

When Tom passed away I told the story
At his wake. How Tom ran his finger

Along the sidewalls of the tomato trailer
Feeling like a mole doctor for popped rivets.

I kept the Jeep story to myself. Later, I poured
half a glass of ale on my floor. This one's for Tom.

THREE ROLLS-ROYCES

The first time we saw a Rolls-Royce
We were hand in hand, remember?
We walked Aspen, our first Siberian,
In summer heat, down to the First Baptist
Church, Charpentier Historic District,
South of Interstate 10 in deep, deep Louisiana.

It was blue and white, or silver maybe,
Shining like an oiled-up hard-on,
Remember? I was teaching English
So what choice did I have but to note
The irony of a Rolls-Royce at a Baptist church. You said:
My Uncle Jasper was a Baptist preacher in Mississippi.
I wanted to sit on its hood and await the owner,
Remember? But Aspen tugged at her leash,
And it was hot, dead noon, Sunday.

The second time was in Presque Isle, Maine.
Right down the road from the three-story ramshackle
We rented. Aspen had died, replaced by Sasha.
The keys were in the Rolls, nighttime, dealership closed,
Like an unholy temptation. The price: two thousand dollars.
The grill intact, worth half that alone, the real wood
Dash waiting to be oiled, its aromas buried under dust.

We might have bought that Rolls…I said:
Picture it: Everyone we know following us down
The street like a Mardi Gras parade. Me in a black
Top hat, you in a sash. What a sight we could be!

The third time we were underground, submerged
In a mall, in Washington, D.C., remember?
Face deep in Asian noodles, some jackass
Was behaving like a jackass, to a teenager
Working the till at Urban Outfitters.

When Jackass left,
        I followed him into the parking structure
        The next street over.
I don't know why
I followed him,
What I expected
I might do. When I came back
        I never told you what happened:

Jackass was driving a black Rolls-Royce.
When he passed me by, I caught a glimpse
in a store window. For a moment it appeared
I was driving. What I never told you was:
I wished I were him.

UNIVERSITY LIFE

He sits in the basement of his dorm
Alone with the spinning heat of HE
Dryers, the humidity of washed linen
Hung like flags of the world, dripping,
He strikes the keys that still function,
The hammerless ones ignored, melody
Sacrificed, occasionally, a stranger appears,
Gathers jeans, underwear from the line.
He plays on, they complement his phrasing,
He does not hear such aubade, a fault
On his mother's side, a family crest.
The stranger shuts the light, a habit,
The dryer keeps time, the laundry line jumps
And jigs, clothes dance as if inhabited.

WATERVILLE, MAINE, OPERA HOUSE

Zooey Deschanel is pouting eighty feet high
And eighty feet away from me. My feet are up
Resting on the eye-level black railing
And as Zooey vacates the screen I peer down
At the wigged and balding heads below.
The balcony is ghostly empty, just me and two
Pimply teenagers stuck to each other at the mouth.
At the top of each aisle a man stands in a suitcoat,
A small earpiece and a thin mic as well, taped to cheek.
They watch the teenage suck-fest and occasionally us,
And it dawns on me they are here to see the movie
Is not taped and distributed ahead of its summer premier.
Zooey is making eyes at me again and for a minute I run
Arias through my mind trying to find one to fit Zooey's
mood. One of the security guards has broken up the teens
and so they watch the movie, mouths wide like river Pike.
Or Perch? I slouch back and stare at the ceiling, the giant
Frescos come alive to the soundtrack. Fat cherubs moving
About in the sky, thankful to break their long-held poses,
Even if they must sing lines someone else is composing.

WE GATHERED BERRIES

All year from farms dotted on maps
From Kennebunk to the rambling hills
Of Aroostook County. Blueberries, nineteen
Miles ahead, we stop along the route
At the insistent wave of every Amish
Boy in a featherlight straw hat. We pay
Their inflated prices willingly
Supporting their families was our summer
Obligation. The air and the fields
Were free, freeing our white shirts
Red and blue from the juices that burst
Each time we pinched off a blackberry
Or dug a stained thumb into the gut
Of a red ripe strawberry, carefully
Unsealing it from its protective green hut.

Then we put them under the knife,
Their blood juice filling the room with summer
Fragrance. The raspberries rated our favorite,
Were easily the most work. Raked into bowls
Atop thick maple batter. A tea cake, crumb-topped
Odoriferous reward. The remaining berries banished,
Anticipating six-month Maine winters, benighted
And frozen in Ziploc freezer bags, gallon size. Future
Reminders of summer gatherings on the bleakest of days.

WEDDING GIFT, 1963

She had all the good silver
Splayed across the table,
A bowl of homemade tarnish
Remover, a recipe she learned
From her mother. The silver
Caused a spark in him.
His mother's
Silver.
Eight-piece set. Soup ladle.
A meat fork he called
"Pitchfork."
The silver was inert,
Came to him in the mail,
Two weeks after the funeral.
Here it was, taking up space,
His wife tending to it
Gently. Each piece losing
Its dioxides, no match
For baking soda, sodium,
The stronger pull of
Aluminum foil.

WEATHER GIRLS

January late and the leotard-dressed weather
girl on that southern cable station giggles,
"Imagine that much snow falling."

She is looking offscreen
at her green screen. Arms flail up and down
through I-95 corridor, a manicured nail stops,

arrows Manhattan, Philadelphia drifts up
toward Boston. My wife and I do not find
weather girl amusing. In any way. We sip

beers and gun insults. Like Elvis.

These weather girls who lunch in Savannah
chortle: "I've never even *seen* measurable snow…"
as Al Roker laments NYC
where snow was close to 70 inches
for the winter.

My wife and I
here in Maine
still can't open our front door

the drifts too high

              (and back to Al in NYC)

"This was a harsh winter," he says,
standing on dry pavement in April.
My wife fires her Schlitz at his face

(Elvis style). I fist back the curtain
stand tippy-toe and peer over the drift.
"It's snowing," I say. My wife squats

next to the RCA and points to where
the crown of Maine would be

if leotard girl would get out of the way. We're
here, she says. Then she whispers,
we're here.

WHAT ARE YOU GOING TO DO

When you get there, when you get to the motel
your wife called from, tears bleeding through
the line, soaking your hand and the curl of your lip?
And why does the image, that moisture on your lip
remind you of the time you cheated at the casino,
remind you of the beautiful young lady working
the valet desk, the one that pressed her coral lipsticked
lip into the waffle holes of her phone, the coral
transferred, wedged, like the imprint of an orange slice.

Why does your mind wander, rather than wonder,
and what would be the point? You have met the man
before, after all, more than once. Good looking. A face
like a friendly moon. You are aware it is all over,
the affair is turning on you. In the long passage of time,
you may come to look like the affair. You will eat frozen
dinners off a TV tray, channel surf, search the house
for traces of her perfume, rummaging her empty drawers,
fingering the corners, finding at first nothing, then scraping
the tongue and groove and finding it after all, the necklace
you made her out of _____, oiled and tight, fisherman's
knots, intricate, waiting all this time for you to discover.

WHAT CHEKHOV SAID ABOUT A MAN, A WOMAN, AND AN ASHTRAY

When I put down Carver's book of collected poems, hours after picking it up, I placed it, some would say oddly, others appropriately, between a book of Chekhov, and Richard Hugo's *The Triggering Town*. What came to me then, wedging its way between the smoky, lingering poems of Carver, and a sudden desire to throw open all the windows of my house, was Hugo's advice that a poet be repetitious and boring, rather than eclectic and various. Had Carver's poems repeated incessantly, even bored me? I decided to open the window, then, something I never did in the throes of winter, and I challenged my memory, that poetic space we all share, to make an image, just one image of what I had read. And I saw a man, a gruff man, and a slender woman, one hand spreading in her hair, the other tapping cigarette ash into an ashtray, and the man was himself unsealing a bottle, and in my head, between my eyes and beneath my forehead was the smell of whiskey and menthol. Outside my window, kids in bright mittens were screaming and running and hurling bright red rubber balls at one another, alternating faces of joy and pain, and birds and squirrels seemed busy with their tasks, and the leaves that had fallen, patched in yellows, reds, and whites, seemed to skitter along through fences, and out past the streets and the rye fields beyond. But here, standing alone with my back to an empty room, I felt only the presence of a man and a woman, and an overwhelming sense of dread.

WHAT IF THE WEATHER CHANNEL FLIPPED

The notion that bigger is better
And we started watching winter weather
From little northern towns like mine?

All the New Yorkers would see
How snow can *actually* inhibit citizens
From going about their days.

I can hear the sympathetic New Yorkers now:
What are they going to *do* with all that snow?
What if Chicagoland was forced to watch

The wind-snow crossing our undivided
Dead-end, deathtrap highways?
Or the L.A. celebrity glitz (so beautiful)

Sat down to chocolate-mint oolong tea
And watched an old lady with an umbrella
Slip and fall on our deathtrap sidewalks?

People here (deathtrap) are afraid to complain
About the weather. We move about our towns,
Content little frozen gerbils in Habitrails.

WHEN THE CASINOS CAME TO TOWN

We stood there and looked like idiots
at the empty car stereo box, tucked,
under our hundred-year-old house
that chartreuse evening in Lake Charles.

How did that get there? you said,
or maybe I did, and we put our heads
together: that cardboard shell crawled
under our house along with the thief,
a port in the storm, the proverbial harbor
in the tempest. Crouched there, we pictured
the thief, how he must have thanked God
for escaping the dampness, the long rye grass,
the lack of basements in southern Louisiana,
his chance to remove the innards from its shell.

In the clearing, I could see the waning moonlight
reflect off exposed crypts, and beyond the cemetery
the booming sounds of the riverboat casino
docking in its slip, back from its thrice-a-day
mandated trip, the gamblers drunk and heavy,
the smoke-filled rooms, the lightness of loss.

WHEN I SPOT YOU

It takes me a minute to realize
You died before the twenty-first century
But there you are. Today you are
At a Baltimore Orioles game, tenth row
Or so, a bratwurst, Natty Bo, an Orioles
Giveaway fisherman's hat.

The last time I saw you walking
Through our dusty local mall
Where you never set a foot
When actually alive
(you hated shopping malls
like all fathers do,
but loved a good ballgame).

You loved to study the Orioles
Schedule the day it appeared
Your red ballpoint pen poised
Ready to strike circles around
The Orioles doubleheaders.

You marked our kitchen calendar
A cartoon version of the Orioles bird
But never knew how I flipped the pages
The perfumed ink knuckling
Over me, staining me with the dates,
Nights before I would wander
The neighborhood in a tight circle
An hour before bed, peering
Into living rooms, stealing signs
From the catchers on the TVs
Unaware, oblivious to everything

Except the coming morning, Mom's
Homemade waffles, my brother and I
Hitting Wiffle balls off the shed, Your
Strong black coffee, the Nova gassed up
My brother and I in the back seat
Pretending you were driving us
From Virginia to Baltimore
In an auto race, the Orioles pregame
Coming in and out on the AM radio.
I caught you stealing a glance
More than once, Mom's arm
Across the bench seat, her fingers
Working your hair like seams.

I must confess to you now,
As I watch you finish your beer
In the tenth row of the ball game,
The Orioles coming to bat in the ninth,
I handle your death by pretending you are not dead.

WHY I WRITE POEMS WHILE MY SONS REHEARSE MUMFORD & SONS

My red dictionary
Is less beautiful than my youngest son's 1976 cherry
Lawsuit Ibanez Double-Axe: A four-string bass atop
Six-strings cuts through the bullshit. My Merriam
Dictionary entraps shit like Pandora's box. My pen
Is not as mighty as his stainless steel Geek Pick.
And my blurry-blue college-lined notebook looks *weirdly* elongated
Lined next to my oldest son's synthesizer keys.
His Moog, with its left-hand side wheels *bends* notes
With ease, as I struggle to find a rhyme or litotes.

Is it because when my sons are off rhythm or pitch
They simply backtrack and fix it?
They simply adjust and play correctly?
I erase a word, add another, a pink nubby
Eraser in my hand, a dulled number two
Ticonderoga in the other.

I tap along with their rhythm, easing from Bowie to
Mumford to Wilco. Switching from electric blue Yamaha
To GoodTime Banjo to acoustic Hummingbird.
Their music floats like ether, and I thrum, thrum, thrum,
To the staccato until my wife calls us all for dinner.
Her homemade aromas mixing with the notes in the air.

HOW ANIMALS ENTER POEMS

I am trying to write a poem
About the mattresses we saw today
Locked lonely behind the Aroostook Centre
Mall glass. Being over fifty years old
We were taking laps
Rather than a friendly tumble!
And on the third pass the black one
Caught your eye. You said *I love the black one*
And *it seems a shame to have to cover its beauty.*
I muttered about their need to sell them
Sticking my hands in my pockets, cold.
You bent to read the tag: *Moonlight Sonata.*

What if the glass doors were unlocked?
Could we have waltzed in and tested the Moonlight?
Would we have rested in the storefront window, in view?
A living Art example of a middle-aged marriage.
Or would you have climbed out of your camel brown coat
Jumped up and down on the beds like a smart black cat
Me chasing you like a dog in heat, a better example
Of a living Art example of middle-aged marriage.

MISSPENT YOUTH IN THE MID-ATLANTIC

Ollie's Trollie's fries with their fennel seeds
A kid-version piña colada soft drink
We would buy just to taste the beach
In winter, cruising Interstate 66 or Route 50
In a T-top Camaro, midnight blue,
"Jessie's Girl" unspooling on the cassette,
Marino's original pizza squares oozing
Down a long-sleeved Sunshine House shirt
(Proof of having been to Ocean City, MD)
Liberty, PA ski tags used as zipper pulls,
Jackets over short pants, the Cicadas return,
Sitting in a friend's (parents') 6 Cyl. Jaguar,
Or 64.5 Mustang, red, a rebel flag pickup,
Dixie horn on the steering wheel, seven
Minutes in the cramped back of a Lambo.
"Hot Rod Hearts" and "Sausalito Summer Nights"
On the dashboard radio, Merriweather Post
Pavilion and RFK Stadium, the Capital Center:
AC/DC shooting cannons for those about to rock.
U2, The Who, Elton John and Randy Newman,
John Cougar on the tour bus watching Letterman,
Their youth long since spent, happy for two hours
To have shared ours, wondering if we would remember.

1979

In the backyard where I once forced the hollow
Of my foot onto the sharp point of a tenpenny nail,
My family and I spent our last night living
In our house, where I had attended seven years of
Francis Scott Key Elementary School
Before moving to the unknown. Seventh grade
Awaited me. Tenth grade awaited my brother.
Unemployment awaited my father.   Night
Held its own secrets, the darkness thicker
Past the broken fence. The porch light, yellow,
Able to cover our makeshift picnic. Watermelon,
Tomatoes, baked beans leftover from the weekend.
Black flies, angry at our swatting, buzzed, cavorted,
Leapt from paper plate to Dixie cup, and back again.
My mother, hot from menopause and anger, watched
My father eat corn from the cob, watched my father
For signs, for signals, for a crack in his façade. My
Brother and I knew only the food and our filling stomachs.
The fireflies blinking in the night, illuminating our lives.

1996

You are under the Louisiana sun
Seven in the morning, mosquitoes sleep.

You are driving a golf cart around a tree
Nursery, turning the sprinklers off and on.

The mist hits your face, you welcome
The spray in such ungodly heat. By nine-

Thirty you are moving fifty-five pound
Plants, sliding their hot black buckets

Across a hotter black fabric tarmac.
Temperature already in the mid-eighties.

You dig three-hundred pound trees
From the ground, root balls sacked

And intact. You coax the trees onto
The Caterpillar's lower teeth. Sweat

Pours through your shirt and underwear.
Break arrives, thirty minutes inside

The cashier's shack. Squeezed between
The cash register and the tiny air conditioner,

Humming and coughing its final breaths.
The watermelon you ate sweats its sugar

Into your hair, and your kidneys scream
At you as you take an air-filled piss.

You spend the afternoon in the greenhouse
Moving a thousand tiny mums to new

Homes, the decades-old box fan hiding
In the corner, its frayed plug dangling

Useless. You reapply fifty sunblock
And adjust the radio, dance along with

Jars of Clay as they sing their song about
Floods, for the ninth time this week.
Inside the temperature steadies
At 90. Outside the forecast is 105.

You find the water pitcher, sun-warmed,
Sprinkle some salt in, you stir, drink. Drink.

You close your eyes, envision your life as a
Northern poet, snowing, like a Frost poem. You

Are unaware how often you will recall this circle
Of Hell. How fondly and genuinely you miss it.

MAYBERRY

When I was a boy I watched Andy Griffith
Propose to his girlfriend on *The Andy Griffith Show.*
Odd how you remember things crystal clear
That should never have been stored,
And still, more odd, shared with others.
How did Andy Griffith know to ask? The question
Bothered me, followed me through my teens,
Got mixed up somehow with an episode of
I Love Lucy. That episode, where Ricky
Buys Lucy a fridge, or a washer, some appliance,
And Lucy goes ape-shit happy. At least as I recall.
Odd, the era before your own is more black & white.

When I became a man I went to the mall alone
In Lake Charles, Louisiana, to the lone jeweler.
A few hundred dollars nervous in my pocket.
You favored emeralds. I favored you. A natural
Emerald seemed the right choice, green for green,
Traded, the ring anxious to be hidden, for months.
The decision no longer what, who, or when, but where.

Mayberry's park, where I remember the proposal,
Remained stuck in my television, memories of Andy
Giving way to where, I found myself alone
With you, at the precipice of Georgetown University.
A stone's throw from my grandmother's house, where
My father grew up, just across Francis Scott Key Bridge.
The scent of Jesuit knowledge. Sanctuary. Generations of
Catholicism, ended with me. The downdraft of the Cherry
Blossoms would not dissipate, nature, its siren call.
I pulled you along the stone walls of campus, down
Potomac Palisades Parkway to the mouth of terror,
The Georgetown steps, where Satan had inhabited a
Jesuit Priest, the devil knocked senseless, by stone.
Past the Exxon station, searching for the where,
Along Canal Road, searching for the where,
Through Georgetown, its high-street fashions,
M Street, where I had wasted my youth, searching.
Following a numbered street to the Chesapeake &
Ohio Canal. I think it was exhaustion, between the
Third and Fourth channel locks, that sat us down, on
Capital Crescent Trail, Georgetown Waterfront Park.
We would so soon be married, betrothed, upriver,
Along the banks of that mighty Potomac, where the river
Widens so deeply, you can barely glimpse the other shore.

HAIKU CROWN

1.
TEACAKE

Richer with berries
Vanilla or chocolate
Cake. Tea on the side.

2.
HUSKY

Pale blue eye, one brown
Different than the other
Like David Bowie

3.
NATIONAL GALLERY

Touching the Manet
Is like entering the past
Except the arrest

4.
SHAKESPEARE

Shall I compare thee
By using the Master's lines
Point out my failings

5.
ONE GUN, ONE BULLET

Would you kill Hitler
Or might you kill his mother
You for writing that

6.
WHEELBARROW

So much depends on
How words are placed in order
A lawsuit or poem

7.
HAIKU 1

You can't say a thing
In just seven syllables
You say everything

8.
HAIKU 2

In five syllables
I can say that I love you
Or tell you to go

9.
HAIKU 3

Beautiful country
"Beautiful America"
Other countries too

10.
PB&J

Two bread slices first
The jam on one bread slice, nice
Peanut butter's last

11.
PRIMARY COLORS (YELLOW PINES)

Red, yellow, blue. Sky
Is blue. Blood is red. Yellow
Is the pine that's not.

12.
POEM FOR MY SONS

Dog days of summer
My sons record instruments
Art is permanent.

NOT ANOTHER POEM ABOUT 22 GRAMS

I have read too many spiritual poems
About dying, and losing 22 grams—
Taken to be someone's soul escaping
Earthly constraint. Centuries, the question
Finally answered, proof of afterlife. Let it be,
I am told. I can't let it go any more
Than I can let go my curiosity about hair.
Perhaps the 22 grams is the weight of oxygen
Expelled at death. Or does one assume oxygen
Bears no weight? Is it the unsightly urine, feces,
That leaks unencumbered, the gaseous fumes
Vacated on death's sweet release? What of this
Lack of curiosity concerning our shorn hair?
Once, I saw a BBC show wherein a woman
Piles up all the food you eat in a month, shows
Its lack of color and health to you, your family.
I want to do the same with every hair I have shed,
Place it on a scale, weigh it, spin the grams
Like sugar, like cotton candy, such monstrosity.

ZURAS THE ETERNAL AS A SONNET

Musty smelling, decade-old comic book,
Paper beaten like pulp, containing pulp
But so much more, for it is Zuras pulp.
I have bought it, brought it, have a look!
My son cannot believe it, thought I mistook
The red-bearded man for my own gestalt.
Puts up his young, large hand, asks that I halt!
I place it before him, snares on my hook—
This is before the film trailer's release,
Before wanton friends, eager high schoolers,
The athletes and student council rulers
Shower my son with jokes most infernal.
These last months of his life with naïve peace,
Watch what you wish, Zuras the Eternal.

ABOUT THE AUTHOR

photo credit: Kelly Zuras

Originally from Arlington, Virginia, Richard Lee Zuras has published two novels, *The Bastard Year* and *The Honeymoon Corruption* (both with Brandylane Publishers, Inc.). Writing poetry informed by confession, Richard has published poems in *Innisfree, South Dakota Review, Red Rock Review, Confrontation, Jabberwock Review*, and *The Great American Wise Ass Poetry Anthology*. He teaches creative writing, film, and general education courses at the University of Maine at Presque Isle, located in northern Maine, where he has lived since 2001. In his spare time, Richard composes song lyrics for his sons' folk/rock band, matches wits with his stubborn dog, and contemplates moving his family to a warmer climate.

CREDITS

"Rogue Soprano" in *Innisfree Poetry Journal*

"House Hunting" in *Confrontation*

"What Chekhov said about a Man, a Woman, and an Ashtray" in *Jabberwock Review*

"Return of Lake Agassiz" in *Nourish*

"Students at a Poetry Reading" in *Upcountry*

"Shallow Grave" in *Poetry Nook*

"Fontanel" in *Red Rock Review*

"First Christmas Without My Father" in *Milkwood Review*

"Weather Girls" in *The Great American Wise-Ass Poetry Anthology*

"The Great Tomato Wreck" in *The Pacific Review*

"Three Rolls-Royces" in *The Pacific Review*

www.ingramcontent.com/pod-product-compliance
Lightning Source LLC
Chambersburg PA
CBHW022108040426
42451CB00007B/175